Crescendo Publishing Presents

Instant Insights on...

RELATIONSHIPS

Love, Talk, Read, *to* Help Your Child Succeed

Celeste Roseberry-McKibbin

small guides. BIG IMPACT.

i

Instant Insights on...
Love, Talk, Read, to Help Your Child Succeed

By Celeste Roseberry-McKibbin, Ph.D., CCC-SLP

Crescendo Publishing, LLC
300 Carlsbad Village Drive
Ste. 108A, #443
Carlsbad, California 92008-2999

www.CrescendoPublishing.com
GetPublished@CrescendoPublishing.com
1-877-575-8814

ISBN: 978-1-944177-98-0 (P)
ISBN: 978-1-944177-99-7 (E)

Printed in the United States of America

Cover design by Melody Hunter

10 9 8 7 6 5 4 3 2 1

What You'll Learn in This Book

This book will help you learn how to love, talk to, and read with your babies and small children using easy, quick strategies to prepare them to succeed in school and achieve their full potential.

It covers all the important questions about language and typical developmental milestones. When should your child say his first word? Put two words together? When should you be concerned, and where do you turn if you are worried that your child might have a language delay?

When our children initiate communication, it is critical to respond immediately with love, affection, and attention. Loving relationships are the cradle of all successful learning. We can begin stimulating our children's language from day one by talking with them, singing, and even reading books. Starting very early in their infancy, we can establish the foundation for conversation.

This book will teach you simple, practical techniques for encouraging your child to use longer sentences with good grammar and new, more sophisticated vocabulary words. You will learn how to read effectively with your child to boost her reading skills for success in school. You will learn why exposure to screens is detrimental to your child's developing language. We'll also discuss the American Academy of Pediatrics' recommendations and summarize the latest research on screen time for children.

Today, expectations of kindergarten children are very high. You want your child to be well prepared, and this book will give you fun and practical strategies for encouraging writing, spelling, and appropriate social skills. You'll understand the benefits of preschool as preparation for entering kindergarten.

You'll get Instant Insights on...

- Developmental milestones of language, what to expect, and when to be concerned
- Responding to your child immediately with love and attention to create a secure emotional foundation
- Talking—creating a conversation using simple, research-based techniques for expanding your child's sentences and vocabulary that you can work into daily routines
- Strategies for reading effectively with your child and increasing her literacy skills
- Specific ways to encourage your child to develop resilience and perseverance so he achieves his full potential
- The consequences of allowing screen time for your child

- Practical strategies for preparing your child for kindergarten by encouraging basic writing, spelling, and social skills

A Gift from the Author

To help you implement the strategies mentioned in this *Instant Insights™* book and get the most value from the content, the author has prepared the following bonus materials:

- A direct link to my YouTube channel with specific how-to demonstration videos of some techniques discussed in the book

- A list of free, fast, easy-to-implement activities designed to build fine motor and sensory skills, along with language skills

You can get instant access to these complimentary materials here:

lovetalkread.com

Dedication

To my precious and wonderful son Mark McKibbin, my angel and inspiration for this book. You are life's best gift from God.

Table of Contents

Getting Started:
Creating a Foundation of Love

My husband and I never thought we could get pregnant, but one day I woke up and there was my precious baby boy. Because Mark was a surprise, I read all I could on how to care for babies. I read in a book that a research study followed babies into their twenties and looked at what variables contributed to happiness in these young adults. It turns out that physical affection shown by caregivers early in life was the number one predictor of adult happiness. Physical affection, devoted attention, and love overcame challenges such as poverty, divorce, substance abuse, and other environmental problems. I realized that my number one priority with my baby was building his foundation with love: responding immediately to his cries and signals, and showering him with physical affection. This would create a secure foundation of attachment, and I could build language skills from there. And, of course, as a speech-language pathologist, I knew I should talk and read with him—and sing, too!

Mark's first year went very well, but then he began getting middle ear infections at twelve months of age. This delayed his speech and language skills early in life. With the work and strategies, I am sharing with you in this book, his verbal skills caught up to and actually exceeded his age level.

But we noticed that Mark had problems with things like cutting, coloring, riding a tricycle, and reading simple words before he started kindergarten. It turned out that he had dyslexia and ADHD, and some neurological problems as well. Mark received several years of occupational therapy, vision therapy, tutoring, and other services to help him catch up to grade level. We worked on his social skills as well.

Today, the little boy who couldn't read, tie his shoes, zip up his jacket, , or make friends is a twenty year-old who was salutatorian of his high school class, graduating with a 4.38 GPA. He is an Honors Political Journalism major at George Washington University in Washington, D.C. Out of 3,000 applicants for this program, he was one of 125 to be chosen. He has worked for Congressmen and Senators (starting when he was fourteen), and has been interviewed on national TV. Mark plans to go to law school eventually and become a social justice attorney.

How did we get from there to here? Statistically, Mark's odds were not good at all. Research shows that a number of children with learning disabilities like Mark's grow up to have life-long social, emotional, and vocational problems. Some even commit crimes and go to prison. So how did that precious baby grow into the little boy with special needs, who is now a brilliant young adult helping guide our country's future?

In this book, I'll share our story and my instant insights. For all the worried parents out there, whether your child is developing typically or has special needs, here are scientifically-supported strategies that really work. I know this from years of direct personal experience. As a Ph.D. university professor, practicing speech-language pathologist, and mom, I see it all. And, I'm here to help. We'll talk about typical language development and discuss free, easy-to-implement, practical strategies for building your child's secure foundation by responding immediately to him with love and attention. I'll share tips for building your child's language skills by talking and reading, and discuss how to prepare her for kindergarten so she is immediately successful.

Let's get started on our journey!

Go to YouTube and type in Celeste Roseberry Love Talk Read. Click on the video entitled *Building Young Children's Vocabulary Through Repetition.*

https://www.youtube.com/watch?v=aLsF7B9wQFE

Your Instant Insights...

- Love, devoted attention, and physical affection early in life are the most important predictors of adult happiness. Respond to your child immediately to build a bond of attachment and trust.

- Even if your child ends up having special needs, addressing them early in life can lead to successful adult outcomes.

- Love-Talk-Read really does work, and it is simple to incorporate these strategies into busy, everyday life.

What to Expect: Typical Developmental Milestones of Language

After Mark was born, I watched him carefully for developmental language milestones. He smiled at six weeks old, cooed at three months, and said his first word by twelve months old. Perfect! But then, middle ear infections set in. By eighteen months old, he should have been saying fifty words and putting two words together. But he was only saying ten words, and was visibly frustrated by his inability to communicate with us. The middle ear infections slowed down his language development considerably. He started having tantrums. It was so hard and frustrating when I didn't understand what my child wanted, and I cried myself to sleep many nights. I knew that Mark should be saying 200 to 300 words by the time he was twenty-four months old, but he was not on track at all. What could I do? We got pressure-equalizing tubes in his ears to heal the ear infections, and that helped immensely. I continued to talk and read to him a great deal, using strategies I share in later chapters.

In this chapter, I share typical developmental milestones of language and what to expect from zero to five years of age. Keep in mind that girls may develop faster than boys, and that children from more relaxed cultures may develop these milestones a little later. If you have questions because your child is not developing as expected, consult your pediatrician. It is also highly recommended that you consult a certified speech-language pathologist for an evaluation and recommendations about next steps (please see *How Does Your Child Hear and Talk* from www.asha.org).

Okay. I know that what follows—lists—can be a little boring. But it's absolutely necessary to know what to expect at various ages, because you can intervene early if your child is not meeting expectations. So, strap yourself in, and here come the lists!

Birth-3 months

Startles in response to loud sounds

Recognizes mother's voice and quiets if crying (my son did that the day he was born—an hour after he was delivered)

Increases or decreases sucking behavior in response to sound

Social smile around 6 weeks (in response to another person)

4-6 months

Moves eyes in the direction of sounds

Makes babbling sounds with many different sounds, including *m, b, p*

Laughs and vocalizes displeasure and excitement

7 months-1 year

Listens when spoken to

Recognizes words for common items like *spoon, ball, juice*

Enjoys games like pat-a-cake and peek-a-boo

Says 1-2 words

Babbles strings of syllables (e.g., babamonigu)

Communicates through gestures (e.g., holding up arms to be picked up, waving)

Shares books with adults as a routine part of life

Can focus on large, bright pictures in a book

By 12 months old, the child should look at and smile at people, reach to be picked up, respond to her own name, enjoy being around people, and make sounds to get attention. She should be saying several words.

1-2 years

Should be saying 10 words by 15 months
Should be saying 50 words by 18 months and putting 2 words together (e.g., "More juice," "Mommy up," "Cocoa bark")
Follows simple directions (e.g., "Roll the ball," "Kiss Daddy")
Points to pictures in a book when named
Likes to turn pages and listen to simple songs, rhymes, and stories
Recognizes certain books by their covers and pretends to read books

By 18 months, the child should interact with familiar adults and children, look at you when you talk, point to pictures or objects to show them to you, wave or say "bye bye," and ask questions ("Where's doggy?" "What's that?").

2-3 years

Should be saying 200-300 words by 24 months old and speaking mostly in 2-3 word phrases (e.g., "Mommy pick up," "Cocoa bark squirrel," "No bath!")
Speech is understood by familiar listeners much of the time
Asks for things by naming them ("Balloon," "Kitty")
Follows 2 consecutive requests ("Get the spoon and put it on the table")
Points to pictures in a book when named

Holds a book correctly
By 24 months, your child should listen to stories, ask for help, take turns talking, and go to people for comfort and affection.

3-4 years

By 3 years old, should be saying 1,000 words
Asks simple questions involving "Who, what, why, where?"
Talks about activities at friends' homes and school
Uses a lot of sentences that have 4 or more words
People outside the family understand most of what the child says
Identifies some letters and matches letters to sounds
Participates in rhyming games
Produces some scribbles that look like letters

By 36 months, your child should talk in short conversations. He should play make believe or pretend games, show emotion, use feeling words like "I love you," and follow 2- to 3-part directions ("Get the book and bring it to me in the kitchen")

4-5 years

By 4 years old, says around 1,600 words
Pays attention to short stories and answers simple questions about them
Understands most of what is said at school and home
Tells stories that stick to the topic
Writes letter-like forms

Understands words that involve time (yesterday, today, tomorrow)

Understands sequencing words (first, next, last)

Names some letters and numbers

Uses grammar like family does

Has friends and is able to share toys and activities

Says most sounds correctly except a few like *r, s, ch, l, th*

Communicates easily with other children and adults

By 4 years of age, your child should play with other children and show interest in people's feelings. He should take part in group activities such as circle time. Your 4-year-old should talk about what happened during the day, and change a message when it is not understood.

By 5 years old, says 2,200-2,500 words

By 5 years of age, your child should have longer conversations and ask a variety of questions. She should talk about her emotions and feelings, and tell simple stories in a logical order. Your child should understand that other people have different thoughts and feelings than she does. She should talk in different ways to different people (e.g., talk to a baby differently than she does a teacher).

As I've said in several parts of this book, a good preschool is one of the best gifts you can give your child. The preschool experience will expand her language and social skills. It will also teach her classroom routines such as lining up, washing hands, and sitting in a circle. All this will prepare her to succeed in kindergarten!

As stated, if you are concerned because your child is not meeting her milestones, start with your pediatrician. Most importantly, take her to a speech-language pathologist who can help you know if your child's development is on track. And if it is not, early intervention can make a world of difference. I know, because early intervention helped my son Mark develop his delayed verbal language skills to make them highly sophisticated. In chapter 4, we will explore more specifics on how to do this.

Your Instant Insights...

- By 1 year of age, babies should be pointing regularly and saying several words.

- By 18 months of age, babies should be saying 50 recognizable words and putting 2 words together into short phrases (e.g., "More juice").

- By 2 years old, children should be saying 200-300 words and speaking in sentences of up to 4 words in length.

Love: Responding to Your Child Immediately

As I said earlier, Mark was a surprise to us. I did know that research showed that within the first six months of life, it is best if we can respond to babies immediately with love and physical affection. I knew that neglecting Mark and letting him cry was not an option—at least for me. More than anything, I wanted him to have a secure foundation. I once heard a speaker say that relationships are the cradle of all learning. Today, Mark is a strong and secure human being who treats me like a queen. We are best friends, and he is a resilient and hardworking college student with a bright future. But it wasn't always easy...

I was raised in the Philippines as the daughter of Baptist missionaries. In Filipino culture, you respond to infants and young children right away, and children often sleep with their parents. We believe in responding immediately to babies and toddlers, and do not believe in letting them "cry it out." So, as a mom here in the U.S., I was very conflicted. Should I let Mark cry it out and sleep in his own room, even if he cried for hours? Wasn't I catering to him and spoiling him if I responded immediately? These were very hard questions for me. I finally decided to go with my gut and upbringing, and the result has been fantastic. Here, I present research-based, scientifically-supported strategies for creating a secure foundation of attachment that will serve your child all his life.

First, research shows us that in the first six months of a baby's life, it is important to respond immediately to their needs. We need to respond with love, warmth, and physical affection. Don't let the baby cry unattended! When we ignore babies, and do not meet their needs, this creates attachment problems—mistrust, insecurity, and fear. Babies learn not to communicate, and they literally give up trying. Thus, not only do babies learn that the world is an unsafe place— they learn that communication does not work to get their needs met. This can create major emotional attachment problems later in life and can negatively impact language skills as well.

When the baby cries, makes noises, or gestures that he wants attention, go to his side as soon as possible. Don't rush in anxiously; be calm, loving, and attentive. Talk to him in a soothing voice. Name his emotions:

> Mark, are you hungry? (pause) Do you need Mommy to feed you? (pause) Here is some milk!

> Uh oh, someone is scared of the dog. (pick him up and hold him close) Is Mark scared of Cocoa? (pause) I've got you. You are with Mommy now.

> Oh, you don't like that wet diaper, do you? (pause) Here, Daddy will change you now. Let's get that wet diaper off you and get a nice dry one on! There we go! All nice and dry! That's a lot better.

After six months of age, if the baby cries, it may be acceptable to speak to him and let him hear your voice before you physically go over to him. Try talking to him soothingly, even if you are a small distance away:

> Mark, honey, Mommy hears you. I love you. I'll be over in a minute. You'll be okay. That's my sweet boy.

> I hear that siren too—that's a big noise! Mommy is here. I love you, and I'll be right over to give you some hugs. That siren was really loud!

When your baby is older—after he turns one—affection and attention are still important. Your child will love and benefit from being hugged, held on your lap, and kissed. But be sensitive; at some point, your child may feel smothered or overwhelmed. Watch carefully for these signs!

When my son was three and could speak in short sentences, I told him that it was okay to let me know if he'd had enough. One day, my sweet child said to me after a long hugfest, "Mommy, no more hugs and kisses, please." That was my cue! I laughed, thanked him for telling me the truth, and gave him some needed physical space. It is very important to help our children learn to set boundaries and feel safe and accepted when they do so.

When children experience love and attention, they develop secure attachment. Attachment creates resilience, and this is a foundation for life. Caregivers who foster warm, nurturing relationships with children foster resilience that protects them from the worst effects of a harsh early environment. We need to be emotionally and physically present and responsive. I'll never forget one day, when I was especially busy and distracted, Mark came up and said, "Mommy, give me you!" I laughed and realized the truth of those words.

Discussing attachment research, Paul Tough (2012) writes, "When mothers scored high on measures of responsiveness, the impact of those environmental factors [poverty, crime, homelessness] seemed to almost disappear. High-quality mothering...can act as a powerful buffer against the damage that adversity inflicts on a child's stress-response system...[With responsive mothering] the effect of all those environmental stressors, from overcrowding to poverty to family turmoil, was almost entirely eliminated...Regular good parenting can make a profound difference for a child's future prospects" (32-33).

The research found that children of responsive mothers were, at one year old, more independent and brave than babies whose cries had been ignored. In preschool, the children of responsive mothers were the most self-reliant. Early attachment creates positive psychological effects that can last a lifetime.

Other research found that attachment status at one year of age was highly predictive of many outcomes later in life. Securely attached children were more socially competent, better able to form close friendships, more resilient, and better able to deal with obstacles later in life.

Before we worry about talking, reading, and writing, the most important thing to focus on is love for and attachment to our children. This is the foundation for everything else.

Your Instant Insights...

- Respond immediately with love and physical affection to your baby's signals— cries, coos, gestures. Immediate, loving, affectionate response builds trust; ignoring your baby fosters suspicion and detachment, which can negatively impact her for the rest of her life.

- Secure attachment early in life is the foundation for success in the future.

- Children who are ignored give up and experience negative effects on language and emotional development, frequently experiencing lifelong problems as adults.

Talk: Building Conversations

Very early in Mark's life, we started working on taking turns. He'd make a noise, I'd respond, and then I'd wait for him to make a noise or gesture in return. Simple conversations, involving give-and-take, began before he even started talking! I talked with Mark constantly. In the car, the park, at meal times—the conversation always flowed. When he became a little older, no matter how tired or busy I was, I worked very hard to have conversations with him and not shoo him away. Despite the fact that he had reading and writing problems in elementary school, his early verbal skills grew quickly. Language testing revealed that at six years of age, his overall spoken language skills were at almost a nine-year-old level. People marveled at his long sentences and sophisticated vocabulary! Today, he is a gifted writer and speaker who was featured several times on national television at the Democratic National Convention in Philadelphia when he was just eighteen.

Talking is preceded by joint attention, or paying attention to the same thing. A child indicates interest in various ways, and we have to be sensitive. A child may cry. She may gaze at an object. She might point, or make noises. The sensitive caregiver understands all these small attempts at communication, and responds immediately and with warmth as often as possible. This builds the foundation for conversation, letting the child know that her attempts to communicate are rewarded with attention and love.

In the old days, we used to believe in the "waterfall of words." In this paradigm, the adult talked as much as possible, regardless of whether or not the child was interested. While the scientific community still believes in talking a great deal to children, we now know that there is something even more effective: responding immediately to what the child is interested in. Research shows these immediate responses encourage early speech and language development.

There are four things to do to establish joint attention and a small conversation: notice what the child is looking at, what she is pointing to, when she vocalizes (makes a noise), or when she uses words. Respond immediately to these cues. Here are some examples:

1. Baby Marissa is in her crib watching her mobile. She is gazing at a sheep. You can notice this and say, "Look at that sheep! She is white and fluffy!"

2. Mom is shopping at Safeway, and ten-month-old Landon is in the cart. He sees a colorful box of Frosted Flakes and points to it. Mom notices him pointing and immediately says, "Look, those are Frosted Flakes with Tony the Tiger. That's what some kids eat for breakfast!"

3. Dad is out with Maria in the stroller, and they pass a neighborhood cat. Dad notices Maria looking at the cat with great interest and saying "Ah! ah!" He immediately says, "I see that white kitty! How pretty! The kitty is wearing a blue collar."

4. Grandpa and Juan are at a local park. Juan laughs and says, "Duck!" Grandpa notices that Juan is looking at a duck some feet away, and says, "That's right, there's a big duck and he is swimming in the pond!"

5. Mommy and Mark are looking at the church directory (yes, that's us. When Mark was one year old, he loved having me name church members!). Mark says, "Who dat?" Mommy says, "That's Gladys. Her name is Gladys Smith."

Again, research has shown that noticing what the child is interested in and responding immediately to the child's interest is even more effective in building language than the "waterfall of words."

We can talk with our infants and small children during routine activities. But it is also helpful, when possible, to create small periods several times a day for special interactions where we focus exclusively on our child (no phones!). These periods can involve reading a book, playing with toys, etc.

An easy, scientifically-supported technique you can use is called extensions. That is where we add words to something the child says. You can do this any time, in any language. Use of extensions adds to a child's vocabulary and definitely helps him use longer sentences. Here are some examples:

> Child: More juice.
> Adult: You want some more grape juice because you're thirsty? Here you go!

> Child: Doggy bark!
> Adult: Yes, the black doggy is barking and wagging his tail.

> Child: Read Thomas now?
> Adult: Yes, we can read your *Thomas the Tank Engine* book as soon as dinner is finished.

Extensions worked well for Mark, and his sentences became long and sophisticated. When he was two years old, we would be at the checkout stand at the store and he'd say, "Thanks, and have a nice day!" The clerk would get whiplash and say to me, "Did that baby just say that?" I'd just smile and thank extensions!

You can start encouraging pointing when the baby is around six months old. Though the baby probably won't start pointing when she is this young, it is good for you to point to things to encourage this important milestone.

We want to use the same vocabulary words over and over in certain routines. Use short, complete sentences and emphasize key words a little more. Use gestures and repetition!

(at the tub) Oh boy! Time for your **bath**! Here's the **bath**! (pointing to bathtub) Now, Daddy has the **soap** (picking up the soap and showing it to the child). The **soap** will get you all clean!

(at mealtime) Time to sit in your **chair**! (pointing to chair) Oh, your **chair** is comfortable. Here's your **cup** (handing cup to the child). Is that Meghan's **cup**? Yes! Now, we will eat **cereal** (pouring cereal into the bowl). Look, this yummy **cereal** is for you.

There are many other free, easy strategies you can use to encourage your child's early language development:

> Teach your child to take turns. Pat-a-cake and peek-a-boo are great games for encouraging this.

> Sing! Use songs with motions.

> Give children chances to put objects in and out of containers, line them up, and move them around while talking about what is going on. You can use boxes, margarine containers, and other simple household items.

> When your child is a little older, stretch—build on the moment and ask follow-up questions that expand the child's thinking and learning. You can say things like "What did you think about that?" "Why do you think....?" "How does that make you feel?"

For preschoolers, help children see how ideas and objects relate to each other. Use words such as *similar, alike, opposite, different,* etc. You can also introduce categories such as *fruits, vegetables, furniture, transportation.* Teaching categories will be very helpful for kindergarten. Introduce the alphabet, numbers, colors, and shapes. Ask more *why* questions that help children think things through and problem-solve. Make books with pictures that your child draws or that you cut out of magazines or get from the Internet. Google images helps! Encourage the child to create a story that you write down.

Preschoolers also enjoy guests such as neighbors, grandparents, and other children who come to visit the house. Encourage children to have conversations with these visitors. Encourage children to engage in cooperative activities with others, such as playing house or putting together a puzzle—activities that promote joint cooperation. Help children put on a puppet show.

Lastly, spend time talking with preschoolers about their feelings. Give them words to describe how they feel. If a child has negative feelings like jealousy or anger, share times when you have felt that way and what you did to feel better. Always reassure children that feelings are not wrong or bad; it is the actions we take that count. Help them find outlets for negative feelings. For example, let them run in the park, jump on a miniature trampoline, or punch a punching bag.

Go to YouTube and type in Celeste Roseberry Love Talk Read. Click on the video entitled *How to Talk to Your Child During Daily Routines.*

https://www.youtube.com/watch?v=FUsoPAIb3A0

Your Instant Insights...

- We start conversations with babies through developing joint attention—noticing what our child is paying attention to and then immediately responding by talking about it.

- When we respond immediately to what our children are interested in, we should emphasize key words and use extensions to add words to what they have just said.

- Teach preschool children basic concepts they will need for kindergarten, and encourage them to engage in cooperative activities and extended conversations.

Talk: Establishing Respectful Behavior

Mark was precious and delightful, but very strong-willed. When he was small, I let him get away with a lot because I literally didn't know what to do. I had been a very compliant child terrified of displeasing adults. But my wonderful little boy was stubborn and often told me "no," insisting on his own way. I didn't want to slap or spank him, but his behavior was sometimes unacceptable and I let him run all over me. Other people noticed and remarked on it! I'll never forget the time when he (at age three) argued with me for so long that I finally said, "We are doing this because I'm the mommy and you're the boy!" He burst into tears and said, "I am not a boy! I'm a superhero!" It was time for things to change.

One day, right after Mark turned three, a friend put a fantastic book in my hand. This book, *Setting Limits with Your Strong-Willed Child*, transformed my relationship with my son from one of conflict and tears to one of respect, obedience, and peace. Our relationship became so much better because he felt safe; my boundaries were strong and non-negotiable. I learned how to use language to help my son think, listen, and problem-solve—and, most of all, obey me. Here is what I learned about using language when my son tested my limits (by the way—it works with adults, too!).

First, I learned that anger doesn't work—consequences do. We can help our young children understand cause and effect. When Mark was small, I had tapes in my car. He loved the Shania Twain tape and I played it a lot. But often, when I wasn't looking, Mark would sneak into my car and unwind my tapes. They were definitely ruined! One day, he destroyed the Shania Twain tape. I said nothing and threw it away. The next day, he asked me to play it. Very matter-of-factly, without anger, I said, "You broke it. You broke the Shania Twain tape. It's all gone." I could just hear the wheels turning in that little blonde head, and he never played with my tapes again. I didn't replace the tape. I let natural consequences teach Mark cause and effect!

Rob MacKenzie, the author of the book mentioned above, says that if you tell a compliant child to do something, they will generally do it to please you. But if you tell a strong-willed child to do something, their very first thought is, "And what will you do if I don't?" That was definitely my son! So, I learned to give him choices with consequences. For example:

> Me: Sweetie, please pick up your toys and put them away.
> Mark: No!
> Me: If you choose to not pick up your toys, you may not watch cartoons after dinner (I made sure he understood). But if you pick up your toys right now, you can watch cartoons. I'm going to count to three. If you have not started picking up your toys by the count of three, no cartoons. One... Two...

If Mark started picking up his toys, I praised him and said, "Good choice! I am so happy that you obeyed me. Now you get to watch cartoons."

If Mark defiantly did not start picking up his toys, I said, "I'm sorry you did not pick up your toys like I asked. You made a choice to not watch cartoons after dinner. I hope you will make a better choice tomorrow." He would cry and start picking up his toys, but it was too late. No cartoons!

Here is another example. We were at Burger King after Sunday school, and Mark positioned himself at the bottom of the play structure's slide. He was spitting at kids as they came down the slide. I told him to stop, but he continued. I said, "I am watching, and if you do that one more time, we are going home right away." Mark loved Burger King, and definitely didn't want to leave. But the next time a child came down the slide, Mark spit at her. I went over (again, not displaying anger) and said, "That's it. I told you no spitting or we would leave. You spit at that girl, and now we are leaving."

Mark began crying loudly and promised not to do it again, begging me to stay. But I picked him up, tucked him under my arm, and carried him to the car. We drove home in silence. The next week when we went back to Burger King, he was much better and never spit again!

I also learned to give Mark time outs. I told him that "Acting mean equals acting mean alone." If he was deliberately being unpleasant or disobedient, he had to go to his room and could not come out until I said it was time. That was very effective.

When Mark would start crying and occasionally have a tantrum, it was so very hard not to give in. But giving in is the worst thing we can do, because children learn that we don't mean business and they can control us. This sets the foundation for conflict, disrespect, and bad behavior in other situations with other people like teachers at school. It is so hard to be strong and hold the line, but it is crucial. I never showed anger when Mark deliberately disobeyed me, but I held the line in all situations and followed through with the promised consequences. It wasn't long before he realized that I meant what I said and was not going to give in. Sometimes we have to do this for several weeks, but eventually children realize that we are in charge, not them. Once more, they feel much safer and happier when they realize we are in control. Too much freedom is not good for children, and it is very unhealthy for them to feel like they control us. As one book said, if we don't tell our children "no," eventually someone will. And hopefully that won't be the police.

Again, our home and our relationship were transformed when I used words, choices, and consequences to teach Mark cause and effect. When things became more harmonious and peaceful, we were able to have so many more happy times together. My little superhero learned that yes, he really was a boy...and Mommy was in charge!

Your Instant Insights...

- Never slap or spank children. Always use words to shape their behavior.

- Set boundaries on your children's behavior by giving clear, understandable choices and consequences. Make sure they understand what you said.

- If your child defies you, don't respond in anger. Follow through with your consequence and do not give in. In time, your child will respect you more, and life will be much happier and more peaceful.

Read: Practical Strategies for Building Pre-Literacy Skills

I had literally read to Mark from day one, and as a baby he loved books—especially *Thomas the Tank Engine*. He went to high-quality preschools, and started kindergarten when he was almost six. Though he had dyslexia and ADHD, we overcame those issues through therapy and lots of hard work. All that reading in early childhood was paying off, and in the third grade, Mark turned a corner and began reading at a fifth grade level. He wrote his own fiction book at the age of eleven. Today, he reads sophisticated books on politics, philosophy, religion, history, and other topics. He is a gifted writer who started working for Senators and Congressmen in his early teen years. Let's hear it for reading *Captain Underpants* at bed time in kindergarten!

It is never too early to start reading; begin the day the baby is born! Books should have bright, colorful pictures and not too much print on one page. Get sturdy books that babies can chew, handle, touch, and even throw.

Children need to see the adults around them enjoying reading. Children do what their role models do. If you are glued to your phone, your child will want the phone! If he sees you enjoying reading books, he will be excited about reading as well.

Digital books are distracting; most experts highly recommend paper. More will be said about this in the next chapter.

Make reading exciting and fun by using silly, dramatic voices. Be expressive! This is especially important for young children with limited attention spans. Read books your child is especially interested in. In kindergarten, my son Mark started hating reading and would have none of it because dyslexia made reading very hard. He would let me read aloud to him, though, and all he wanted to hear was *Captain Underpants* stories and Bible stories with bad guys (there are plenty of those!). Oh, and he liked the *Dumb Bunny* (by Dav Pilkey) books as well. Sound effects and funny voices kept him attentive and engaged.

I kept reading aloud to Mark, even after reading became easier for him. This helped him enjoy books that were beyond his independent reading level and expanded his vocabulary by exposing him to new words.

Make reading a priority. Bedtime stories are especially good, because they help children wind down and relax. Make a special time for snuggling before they go to sleep. Sometimes, children will want the same book over and over—that's fine! Mark's favorite bed time stories as a very young child were *Good Night Moon* and *The Big Red Barn*.

Help your child figure out new vocabulary. Encourage your child to look at illustrations and pictures to figure out new words, but do supply the meaning if she starts getting frustrated.

As stated, be willing to read the same books over and over—but attempt to introduce new ones once in a while.

Take your child to the local library. Our library had a sign-up sheet where you could register to read with Delilah the Dog. Mark just loved this, and it was very helpful in the early years when he was struggling with dyslexia.

An easy way to remember how to read with your child is to CARE: Comment, Ask Questions, Respond, Extend (add words). You can read the actual book and CARE, or just look at the pictures and CARE. Either way, it's effective.

> Adult: Look at Thomas the Tank Engine going down the track. (Comment)

Adult: Where is he going? (Ask a question)

Child: He's going to see James.

Adult: Yes! He likes to see his friend James, who is the orange train! (Respond and Extend)

Adult: Oh boy, I think James is glad to see him. (Comment)

Child: James happy.

Adult: James is happy because Thomas is his friend and they like having fun together. (Respond and Extend)

Here are some more specific ideas for building your child's early reading skills (google *Sacramento State Literacy Connection*):

Before you start reading a book, look at the pictures and talk about them. Build pre-literacy skills by asking your child:

1. How do you hold a book?
2. Where is the cover?
3. Who is the author?
4. What do you think the book is going to be about?
5. Can you point to the first page?
6. Can you point to the first word?

7. Will you turn the pages with me while we read?

Build on the child's previous knowledge. For example, if the story is about Dogzilla, you can say "Do you have a dog? Do you know anyone who has a dog?" In another example, "Look at that red fire engine. It has four wheels, just like a car. What does your Daddy's car look like?"

During reading, ask questions such as:

1. Where should I read next?
2. Where is the page number?
3. Why did the character do that?
4. What do you think is going to happen next?
5. How does this character make you feel?

After reading, review the story by asking questions such as:

1. What was the story about?
2. What happened in the story?
3. How did the story end?
4. What was your favorite part of the story?
5. Which picture did you like best? Why?

Start building your child's phonological awareness skills—awareness of how words sound. The very best way to do this is through rhyming, and I highly recommend Dr. Seuss books! It's never too early to build print awareness skills—awareness of how words look. An easy way to do this is to start by having your child track print, or put his finger under each word as it is read. You yourself can put your finger under each word as you read. In chapter 7, we'll say more about building phonological awareness and print skills.

Go to YouTube and type in Celeste Roseberry Love Talk Read. Click on the video entitled *Reading Picture Books with Toddlers.*

https://www.youtube.com/watch?v=fAYBmNDl EBo&t=58s

Also check out the video entitled *How to Read to Your Child with Care.*

https://www.youtube.com/watch?v=kjiPMW M3i00&t=53s

Your Instant Insights...

- Read to your baby from day one. Use colorful, bright, interesting books with fun textures.

- Be sure to CARE: Comment, Ask Questions, Respond, Extend.

- Remember to be a role model by reading yourself. Children imitate the actions of the adults around them!

Skyping with Grandma: To Allow or Not to Allow Screen Time?

We very carefully kept Mark away from TV until he was three years old, at which time I began allowing Disney and Bible Man movies. I always watched and discussed the movies with him. Growing up, he was not allowed to play video games. This made it very hard socially with other boys at times, but Mark knew I loved him enough to keep him away from those games. I explained that they were bad for his brain, but we did a lot of other fun activities. Today, Mark proficiently uses his phone and is a whiz at technology, including website-building and social media. He has helped our Sacramento mayor boost his social media profile. Mark is incredibly creative and funny, and has thanked me many times for keeping him away from video games and phones when he was small.

The American Academy of Pediatrics (2018) states:

- For children younger than 18 months, avoid use of screen media other than video chatting.

- Parents of children 18 to 24 months of age who want to introduce digital media should choose high-quality programming, and watch it with their children (joint media engagement) to help them understand what they're seeing.

- For children ages 2 to 5 years, limit screen use to 1 hour per day of high-quality programs. Parents should co-view media with children to help them understand what they are seeing and apply it to the world around them.

- Be sure to place consistent limits on the time spent with screens.

The American Academy of Pediatrics has a Family Use Plan. You can go online and type in information about your children (e.g., their ages) and the website will create an individualized plan tailored to your child's individual needs. Go to

https://www.healthychildren.org/English/media/Pages/default.aspx.

Recent research using sophisticated neural imaging techniques shows us that excessive screen exposure can neurologically damage a young person's developing brain in the same way cocaine addiction can. In one author's words, we are "giving digital morphine to kids" (Kardaras 2016). Screens have been called "electronic cocaine," and addiction has skyrocketed in the U.S. and other countries around the world. Childhood obesity and sleep problems abound.

Stillman and Stillman (2017) tell us that almost half of Millennials are now parents themselves. There is a small but growing trend for these young parents to limit technology with their children, as the parents recognize the negative effects that technology can have. As Stillman and Stillman say, who knew that crayons and play dough would make a comeback?

It takes great discipline, time, and, yes, sacrifice to interact with our children instead of letting technology babysit them. I have been that mom with people glaring at me and giving me dirty looks over my son Mark's behavior in public when he was little. I could just read the "Bad mom!" thought bubble hovering over their heads. In those moments, I would have paid $1,000 cash for a phone or other device to quiet my child down in public. I get it. But interacting with our children instead of using a screen to quiet them pays huge dividends in the end.

We were on a plane to Alaska, and I'll never forget a young mom with a very hyper one-year-old boy who wanted to run the plane aisles for hours. Even I would have brought out a phone in desperation, but this strong, self-disciplined mom was having none of it. She took out some blue masking tape and allowed her boy to tear it into little pieces and stick the pieces on the back of the seat in front of him (yes, she cleaned it up afterward). She had a vast array of real books and stuffed animals. She talked, read, played, and sang—for several hours. I just wanted to cheer. She is a hero in my book, and though she was very ragged by the end of the trip, her child benefitted from love, attention, and hands-on interaction at great cost to his mother.

Current wisdom tells us that the less screen time, the better—especially before the age of five. However, if we choose to let our young children have screen time (e.g., TV, phones, iPads), we should always make sure there is joint media engagement—we need to watch the screens with our children and discuss what is happening. Screens should never, ever be used as babysitters!

J. Ma et al. (2017) studied 1,077 children whose average age was eighteen months old. The researchers found that there was a significant correlation between time that the subjects spent with handheld devices (e.g., phones) and expressive language delay. They concluded that small children who have more handheld screen time are at increased risk of expressive language delays.

We know that it is not good to expose infants and young children to smart phones. But are children impacted by their parents' phone use? A recent study linked parental use of smart phones to misbehavior in children. Author Brandon McDaniel from Illinois State University has been researching technology's intrusion into face-to-face communication and relationships. He found that the more parents spent time on their phones, the more children acted out in tantrums, restlessness, and hyperactivity. McDaniel emphasizes that parents shouldn't feel guilty about needing their phones; however, they need to watch how often they pull out their phones when their young children are around.

Many parents have wondered if it is okay to use electronic books instead of paper or print books with their babies and young children. Recent research about use of electronic books reveals that young children show better focus and comprehension when parents use print books, not ebooks. Scientific studies have proven that ebooks are distracting to young children. While ebooks initially attract and engage young children more readily, print books still win in terms of children developing better vocabularies, sentence structure, and story comprehension. Ebooks may be useful in elementary school and beyond, but their use with young children is discouraged.

Go to YouTube and type in Celeste Roseberry Love Talk Read. Click on the video entitled *How to Build Literacy Through Talking About Pictures in a Book.*

https://www.youtube.com/watch?v=Dtjdx QZuvy4&t=17s

Your Instant Insights...

- The American Academy of Pediatrics has come up with recent guidelines that discourage use of screens before eighteen months of age, except for video chatting.

- Screen time with small children should be very limited. When it is allowed, there needs to be joint media engagement where parents watch with children and discuss what they have seen.

- Current research discourages the use of electronic books with young children, showing that print books increase story comprehension and vocabulary skills and are overall superior to ebooks.

School, Here I Come: Preparing Your Child for Kindergarten

Because Mark was an only child, I knew he needed to socialize. From birth to three years old, he was in a small home care environment. When Mark turned three, I realized this was not enough and placed him into a larger preschool, which also had an elementary after-school program. Wow, did his language skyrocket! What a difference! And he learned about lining up, waiting his turn, sitting in circle, listening, and making friends. I'll never forget going to pick him up one day and seven girls were lined up at the fence, waiting to say goodbye to him. Not bad for an only child!! Right before kindergarten, we put Mark in Montessori. This was honestly one of the best moves I ever made. The teachers worked diligently on his reading, writing, spelling, and phonics. He learned self-discipline and made friends.

Let's talk about preschool. Should you do it? Anecdotally, here is what I have noticed as a speech-language pathologist. The kindergarten children who have never been to preschool have a rocky road ahead of them indeed, and boy, do they stand out! They have no idea how to line up, sit in a circle, pick up their toys, share with other children, and a thousand other small things we take for granted. We tend to focus on academics: Can the child read, write, spell, do simple math?

All of those skills are built upon a foundation of knowing how to behave in the classroom—what some authors have called the "hidden curriculum." When the teacher asks you to do something, you obey immediately; you don't wander off and do your own thing! But a child with no preschool background does not know that, and often is not even ready to learn. Preschool teaches those "hidden curriculum" skills.

My son Mark, having ADHD, interrupted a lot as a preschooler. He came home and told me that Miss Tonya at Montessori would say to him, "Mark, we're not talking about that right now." She would shut down his extraneous comments and keep talking about the topic at hand. Mark needed that! His kindergarten teacher sure wasn't going to tolerate interruptions and deviations from the topic!

As an only child, Mark also needed to learn to do what teachers told him without arguing. I'll never forget a long argument we had when he was three years old—I mentioned this in a previous chapter. He wanted something that I wouldn't give him (probably ice cream before dinner), and finally, in frustration, I said, "We're doing it this way because I said so. I'm the Mommy and you're the boy!" His little face crumpled into tears. "I am not a boy! I'm a superhero!" My little superhero clearly needed to learn how to relate properly to authority figures! Preschool taught him how to obey persons in authority.

Placing your child in a high-quality preschool is the best gift you can give him to prepare him for kindergarten. What else can you do to get him ready, especially in terms of literacy skills?

Phonological awareness, mentioned in chapter 6, is the awareness of the sound system of a language. We said that rhyming is the foundation for this. Here are other skills, listed in a hierarchy, that you want to help your child develop before she goes to school:

1. Count the number of words in a sentence
2. Count the number of syllables in a word (clapping is very helpful)
3. Count the number of sounds in a word
4. Identify the first sound in a word
5. Identify the last sound in a word

A wonderful website that helps with these skills is www.starfall.com. I used it with my own son in kindergarten.

We discussed print awareness skills in chapter 5. Before our children start kindergarten, we can teach them to:

1. Display interest in reading and sharing books

2. Identify the front and back of the book

3. Identify the top and bottom of the page

4. Look at the book while turning the pages from left to right

5. Identify the title on the front cover

6. Identify titles of favorite books

7. Distinguish between pictures and print on a page

8. Know where the story begins in the book

9. Identify letters that occur in their own names

10. Print the first letter of their name

11. Recite the alphabet

12. Point to the first and last letter in a word

13. Differentiate uppercase from lowercase letters

14. Use terms such as letter, word, alphabet

15. Respond to common environmental signs (e.g., stop, restroom signs)

We can also work on simple writing skills with children. Writing depends on fine motor movements of the hand, wrist, and fingers. Mark had a great deal of trouble with writing when he was little, and these ideas helped:

1. Make sure your child has plenty of opportunities to scribble, color, and paint. Make free use of crayons, paint, and sidewalk chalk.

2. Activities involving clay and play dough help develop fine motor skills.

3. Have your child trace letters with her finger in clay, playdough, or salt.

4. When your child is reading or watching TV (not too much!) she can squeeze a squishy ball to strengthen the muscles of her hands and fingers.

5. Encourage writing notes and letters to friends and family members. Remember: Perfection is not necessary, but the attempt to write is very important.

Continue to read with your child, providing many different books about different topics. As she gets a little older, you can add informational books to her repertoire. When children are small, we love to read them stories. Stories are terrific, but kindergartens these days place a great deal of emphasis on reading for information. My son loved *Bob the Builder* books as a preschooler. We read about dump trucks, cement mixers, and other topics. I love Byron Barton books, which are simple and colorful informational books about planes, trains, and other fascinating topics. We can read these informational books with children and ask questions about what they have learned. This will greatly help in preparing them for kindergarten.

Lastly, as your child's language becomes more sophisticated, you can prepare him for school by encouraging what Stanford researcher Dr. Carol Dweck calls a growth mindset. She encourages parents to not say things like, "You're so smart!" (person praise). Instead, she recommends process praise—praising children for effort and hard work. I discovered Dr. Dweck's research when Mark was around nine years old, and it dramatically changed the way I praised him. Here are things you can say to encourage your child to be more perseverant and resilient, relying on effort and hard work rather than innate talent:

> You worked very hard on that. I'm proud of you.
> That took a lot of effort! Way to go!
> You got a good grade because you spent a lot of time working on that picture.
> I love how hard you are trying. Trying hard is the most important thing.

Dr. Dweck explains that when we praise children for innate qualities (e.g., "You're so smart!"), we set them up for failure if they don't succeed. They feel like they failed because they were not really smart, and this makes them insecure. Process praise about effort works wonders. I know, because I tried it and had incredible success with my own child. I stopped telling Mark he was smart. I praised him for hard work, effort, and perseverance. I am confident that this is a major reason he is so successful as a young adult.

Go to YouTube and type in Celeste Roseberry Love Talk Read. Click on the video entitled *Responding with CARE: Comment, Ask Questions, Respond, Extend.*

https://www.youtube.com/watch?v=NoRD DsjuZy8&t=22s

Click also on the video entitled Fostering Print Awareness in Preschool Children.

https://www.youtube.com/watch?v=QU1tDWHgy0Y

Your Instant Insights...

- High-quality preschool is one of the very best gifts you can give your child. Be sure to choose a place that emphasizes creative play as well as reading and writing!

- Begin addressing phonological and print awareness skills, developing fine motor skills for writing as well.

- Don't tell your child, "You're so smart!" Praise effort, hard work, and perseverance to build a more resilient child who is not afraid of failure.

Putting It All Together

All of us want our children to succeed and have a bright future. Around our globe, this is every parent's universal desire. We want our children to have a strong start, for we know that this excellent foundation leads to a life of success and happiness.

Though my husband and I did all the right things and then plenty more, something was wrong with our beautiful baby. Dyslexia, ADHD, and neurological problems were not what we expected from the child of two parents with their doctorates. But time, lots of therapy, and patience helped our son succeed and become the wonderful twenty-year-old he is today. We implemented virtually every strategy you read about in this book. I've shared the how-tos of our journey, and know that they can work for you as well.

It has been so gratifying to see Mark go from a shy, insecure little boy who couldn't read, write, or tie his shoes to a confident, brilliant, successful college student who has worked for Senators and Congressmen and wants to go to law school. When I see him deep in the middle of a thick book on American history or read his philosophy class college essays, I am transported back to that night when my six-year-old tearfully told me as he cried himself to sleep, "I'm stupid—I'm a loser—I kill myself." How did we get from there to here?

Starting on day one, I responded to Mark with love. I did not let him "cry it out," but rather attended to his needs immediately with love and affection. I gave him lots of hugs and kisses, and held him a lot. I talked to him a great deal, noticing what he was interested in and responding to that in the moment. I so clearly remember using extensions constantly—both during daily routines and special times like reading a book before bed. When he said something, I'd add words. When he said, "*Good Night Moon*, Mommy?" I'd say, "Yes, we will read your book *Good Night Moon* before you go to sleep." Mark's early verbal skills were very highly developed, and I know my use of extensions was key.

We read to Mark every single day. Even when he began to dislike reading for a few years because it was so hard for him, we continued reading aloud. I learned how to use funny voices and be entertaining and engaging!

I also learned how to set boundaries with Mark by giving him choices and consequences. When he defied me, I did not show anger and yell at him or slap or spank him. He was not allowed to negotiate. I followed through with consequences and life became much happier and more peaceful.

We put Mark in stimulating preschools with lots of outdoor activities and literacy activities as well. We saw his verbal and social skills skyrocket as he, our only child, spent time learning to relate to children from a variety of cultural backgrounds and age levels. His first best friend ever (when he was one year old) was Mexican; his other best friend was Chinese and spoke only Mandarin when he came to Montessori. We joke that Ryan learned English to defend himself with his assertive best friend Mark!

Carol Dweck's growth mindset research dramatically altered the way I praised Mark. Gone were statements such as "You're so smart" and "Wow, you're a great artist!" These were replaced by process praise, which emphasized effort and perseverance. I have often thought that given Mark's special challenges such as dyslexia, we would be at a very different place today without process praise. He struggled for years with things that came easily to other children. I so clearly remember him crying on more than one occasion and saying, "Mommy, why are things so easy for the kids and so hard for me?" I would take him in my arms and tell him how special he was, and that he was learning to work harder than everyone else. I told him that God wanted him to do special things someday, and that his problems were helping him to learn to work extra hard. Mark knew the word "perseverance" very early in life.

Today, he is a resilient, happy, and incredibly industrious twenty year old with an extremely bright future. He goes to school at George Washington University in Washington, D.C. There were 3,000 applicants for the Honors Program in the School of Media and Public Affairs, and Mark was one of 125 that were chosen. I am so thankful.

And I wish you the very best for yourself and your own child. If you are struggling, know that you are not alone and that there is hope. Don't be afraid to seek special help and support if your child needs it. Mark had occupational therapy for two years, vision therapy for one and a half years, and tutoring at various points from preschool through high school. He has seen a professional therapist to help cope with issues that arise from having ADHD.

Love, Talk, Read really does work. Simple strategies such as those I've described in this book are scientifically supported and have worked so well for my own child. Be consistent and persistent, and your efforts will pay off. And remember, as three-year-old Mark said, "Give me you." Your love is the best gift of all.

Your Instant Insights...

- It all starts with love and attachment— creating a secure foundation by responding immediately to babies and providing lots of physical affection.

- We build our children's language skills by talking to them and responding instantly to their initiations.

- We provide opportunities for our children to read, write, and socialize to prepare them for school, while minimizing screen time as much as possible.

About the Author

Celeste Roseberry-McKibbin received her Ph.D. from Northwestern University. She is a Professor of Communication Sciences and Disorders at California State University, Sacramento. Dr. Roseberry is also currently a part-time itinerant speech-language pathologist in the San Juan Unified School District, where she provides direct services to students from preschool through high school. She has worked in educational and medical settings with a wide variety of clients, ranging from preschoolers to geriatric patients. She enjoys volunteering to help homeless persons in her community.

Dr. Roseberry's primary research interests are in the areas of assessment and treatment of culturally and linguistically diverse students with communication disorders, as well as service delivery to students from low-income backgrounds. She has more than 70 publications, including 16 books, and has made over 370 presentations at the local, state, national, and international levels. Dr. Roseberry is a Fellow of the American Speech and Hearing Association (ASHA), and winner of ASHA's Certificate of Recognition for Special Contributions in Multicultural Affairs. She received the national presidential Daily Point of Light Award for her volunteer work in building literacy skills of children in poverty. She lived in the Philippines as the daughter of Baptist missionaries from ages six to seventeen.

Connect with the Author

Websites:
www.lovetalkread.com
www.hhs.csus.edu/homepages/SPA/Roseberry

Email:
celeste@csus.edu

Address:
Department of Communication Sciences and Disorders
Sacramento State University
Folsom Hall, 7667 Folsom Blvd.,
Sacramento, CA 95826

Phone:
(916) 278-6601

Social Media:
Facebook: Love Talk Read
LinkedIn: Celeste Roseberry
Twitter: @love_talk_read
Instagram: Love Talk Read
YouTube: Celeste Roseberry (Love Talk Read)

Other Books by this Author

Roseberry-McKibbin, C. 2018. *Multicultural children with special language needs: Practical strategies for assessment and intervention.* 5th ed. Oceanside, CA: Academic Communication Associates.

Roseberry-McKibbin, C., and M.N. Hegde. 2016. *An advanced review of speech-language pathology: Preparation for Praxis and comprehensive examination.* 4th ed. Austin, TX: Pro-Ed.

Roseberry-McKibbin, C. 2014. *Increasing oral and literate language skills of children in poverty.* Professional development continuing education program for the American Speech-Language Hearing Association. Rockville, MD: American Speech-Language-Hearing Association.

Roseberry-McKibbin, C. 2013. *Increasing the language and academic skills of children in poverty: Practical strategies for professionals.* 2nd ed. San Diego, CA: Plural Publishing, Inc.

Karanth, P., C. Roseberry-McKibbin, and P. James. 2017. *Intervention Manual for Prerequisite Learning Skills: Practical Strategies.* San Diego, CA: Plural Publishing.

Karanth, P., C. Roseberry-McKibbin, and P. James. 2017. *Intervention for Preschoolers with Cognitive,*

Social, and Emotional Delays: Practical Strategies. San Diego, CA: Plural Publishing.

Karanth, P., C. Roseberry-McKibbin, and P. James. 2017. *Intervention for Toddlers with Cognitive, Social, and Emotional Delays: Practical Strategies.* San Diego, CA: Plural Publishing.

Karanth, P., C. Roseberry-McKibbin, and P. James. 2017. *Intervention for Preschoolers using Augmentative and Alternative Communication: Practical Strategies.* San Diego, CA: Plural Publishing.

Karanth, P., C. Roseberry-McKibbin, and P. James. 2017. *Intervention for Toddlers using Augmentative and Alternative Communication: Practical Strategies.* San Diego, CA: Plural Publishing.

Karanth, P., C. Roseberry-McKibbin, and P. James. 2017. *Intervention for Preschoolers with Gross and Fine Motor Delays: Practical Strategies.* San Diego, CA: Plural Publishing.

Karanth, P., C. Roseberry-McKibbin, and P. James. 2017. *Intervention for Toddlers with Gross and Fine Motor Delays: Practical Strategies.* San Diego, CA: Plural Publishing.

Karanth, P., C. Roseberry-McKibbin, and P. James. 2017. I*ntervention for Preschoolers with Communication Delays: Practical Strategies.* San Diego, CA: Plural Publishing.

Karanth, P., C. Roseberry-McKibbin, and P. James. 2017. *Intervention for Toddlers with Communication Delays: Practical Strategies.* San Diego, CA: Plural Publishing.

Acknowledgements

I would like to thank Robbin Simons and Shayna Rohrig of Crescendo Publishing for this wonderful opportunity to share my literacy vision with a wider audience.

Thanks, and lots of love to Dr. Elaine Fogel Schneider for introducing me to Crescendo and facilitating this relationship.

Most of all, I thank God, my heavenly Father for the gifts of life, health, and the chance to communicate this vision to the world.

Resources

www.lovetalkread.com

Sac State Literacy Connection (detailed
instructions in multiple languages about
building your child's literacy skills)
http://csus.edu/hhs/csad/research/
literacy-connection.html

Vroom (ideas for language development)
http://www.joinvroom.org/parents

Developmental milestones in different languages
www.cdc.gov/ncbddd/actearly/milestones

American Academy of Pediatrics
www.asha.org

7 Strategies for Raising Calm, Inspired, and
Successful Children
http://www.askdrelaine.com

Create your own Family Media Plan
https://www.healthychildren.org/
English/media/Pages/default.aspx

Good toys for young children
http://www.naeyc.org

Tips for Attachment Parenting
http://www.attachmentparenting.
org/principles/principles.php

Suggestions for growth and development for preschoolers
http://kidshealth.org

Easy, practical activities for developing early literacy skills
http://www.earlyliteracylearning.org

Popular resource for educational toys
http://www.melissaanddoug.com

Ideas for developing school readiness
http://main.zerotothree.org

References

Apel, K., and J. Masterson. 2012. *Beyond baby talk: From speaking to spelling—A guide to language and literacy development for parents and caregivers.* Rockville, MD: American Speech-Language-Hearing Association.

Bardige, B.S. 2009. *Talk to me, baby! How you can support young children's language development.* Baltimore: Paul H. Brookes Publishing.

Duckworth, A. 2016. *Grit: The power of passion and perseverance.* New York: Scribner.

Dweck, C.S. 1996. *Mindset: The new psychology of success.* New York: Random House.

Fowler, W. 1995. *Talking from infancy: How to nurture and cultivate early language development.* Cambridge, MA: Center for Early Learning and Child Care.

Gold, J. 2015. *Screen-smart parenting: How to find balance and benefit in your child's use of social media, apps, and digital devices.* New York: Guilford Press.

Kardaras, N. 2016. *Glow kids: How screen addiction is hijacking our kids—and how to break the trance.* New York: St. Martin's Press.

Ma, J., M. van den Heuvel, J. Maguire, P. Parkin, and C. Birken. 2017. *Is handheld screen time use associated with language delay in children*? Paper presented at the annual Pediatric Academic Societies Meeting, San Francisco, CA.

McDaniel, B.T., & Coyne, S.M. 2016.*Technology interference in the parenting of young children: Implications for mothers' perceptions of co-parenting.* The Social Science Journal, 53(4), 435-443.

MacKenzie, R.J. 2001. *Setting limits with your strong-willed child: Eliminating conflict by establishing CLEAR, firm, and respectful boundaries.* New York: Three Rivers Press.

Marklund, U., E. Marklund, F. Lacerda, and I. Schwarz. 2015. "Pause and utterance duration in child-directed speech in relation to child vocabulary size." *Journal of Child Language* 42: 1158-1171.

Schneider, E.F. 2016. *7 strategies for raising calm, inspired, and successful children.* Carlsbad, CA: Crescendo Publishing.

Stillman, D., & Stillman, J. 2017. Gen Z @ work: How the next generation is transforming the workplace. New York: HarperCollins Publishers.

Tough, P. 2012. How children succeed: Grit, curiosity, and the hidden power of character. New York: Mariner Books.

Van Kleeck, A. 2006. *Sharing books and stories to promote language and literacy.* San Diego, CA: Plural Publishing.

About Crescendo Publishing

Crescendo Publishing is a boutique-style, concierge VIP publishing company assisting entrepreneurs with writing, publishing, and promoting their books for the purposes of lead-generation and achieving global platform growth, then monetizing it for even more income opportunities.

Check out some of our latest best-selling AuthorPreneurs at http://CrescendoPublishing.com/new-authors

About the Instant Insights™ Book Series

The *Instant Insights™ Book Series* is a fact-only, short-read, book series written by EXPERTS in very specialized categories. These high-value, high-quality books can be produced in ONLY 6-8 weeks, from concept to launch, in BOTH PRINT & eBOOK formats!

This book series is FOR YOU if:

- You are an expert in your niche or area of specialty

- You want to write a book to position yourself as an expert

- You want YOUR OWN book – NOT a chapter in someone else's book

- You want to have a book to give to people when you're speaking at events or simply networking

- You want to have it available quickly

- You don't have the time to invest in writing a 200-page full book

- You don't have a ton of money to invest in the production of a full book – editing, cover design, interior layout, best-seller promotion, etc.

- You don't have a ton of time to invest in finding quality contractors for the production of your book – editing, cover design, interior layout, best-seller promotion, etc.

For more information on how you can become an *Instant Insights™* author,
visit **www.InstantInsightsBooks.com**

Made in the USA
Columbia, SC
09 February 2018